Dinosaur Graveyards in North America

by Grace Hansen

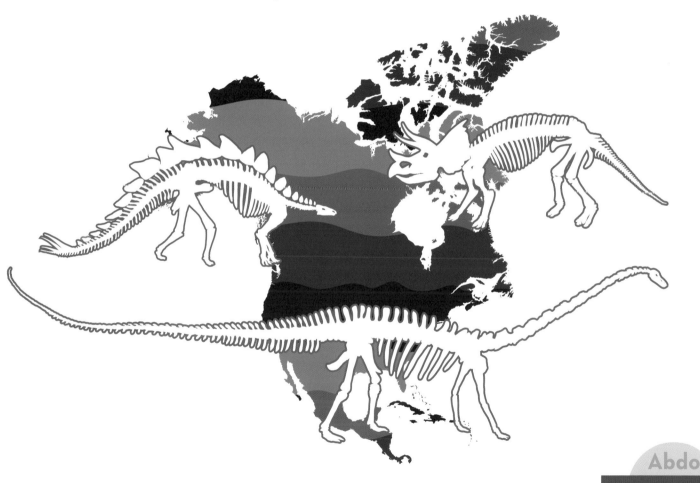

Abdo
DINOSAUR GRAVEYARDS
Kids

Abdo Kids Jumbo is an Imprint of Abdo Kids
abdobooks.com

abdobooks.com

Published by Abdo Kids, a division of ABDO, P.O. Box 398166, Minneapolis, Minnesota 55439.
Copyright © 2022 by Abdo Consulting Group, Inc. International copyrights reserved in all countries.
No part of this book may be reproduced in any form without written permission from the publisher.
Abdo Kids Jumbo™ is a trademark and logo of Abdo Kids.

Printed in the United States of America, North Mankato, Minnesota.

102021

012022

Photo Credits: Getty Images, iStock, Science Source, Shutterstock,
©Jim, the Photographer p13 / CC BY 2.0, ©Rodney p15 / CC BY 2.0

Production Contributors: Teddy Borth, Jennie Forsberg, Grace Hansen
Design Contributors: Candice Keimig, Pakou Moua

Library of Congress Control Number: 2021940141

Publisher's Cataloging-in-Publication Data

Names: Hansen, Grace, author.

Title: Dinosaur graveyards in North America / by Grace Hansen

Description: Minneapolis, Minnesota : Abdo Kids, 2022 | Series: Dinosaur graveyards | Includes online
    resources and index.

Identifiers: ISBN 9781098209483 (lib. bdg.) | ISBN 9781098260194 (ebook) | ISBN 9781098260545
    (Read-to-Me ebook)

Subjects: LCSH: Dinosaurs--Juvenile literature. | Fossils--Juvenile literature. | North America--Juvenile
    literature. | Paleontology--Juvenile literature. | Paleontological excavations--Juvenile literature.

Classification: DDC 567--dc23

Table of Contents

Dinosaurs of North America 4

Dinosaur Park Formation 8

Hell Creek Formation 10

Woodbury Formation 12

Big Bend 14

Morrison Formation 18

Some Major Dinosaur Groups . . 22

Glossary 23

Index 24

Abdo Kids Code 24

Dinosaurs of North America

Dinosaurs lived between 245 and 66 million years ago. After a dinosaur's death, its remains could turn to fossil if the conditions were perfect. This process takes more than 10,000 years!

Every continent has dinosaur fossils, including North America. Fossils are often found in **rock formations**. Some formations hold more remains than others!

North America

Europe

Africa

South America

Dinosaur Park Formation

The Dinosaur Park Formation is in Alberta, Canada. It is known for a few unique dinosaurs.

8

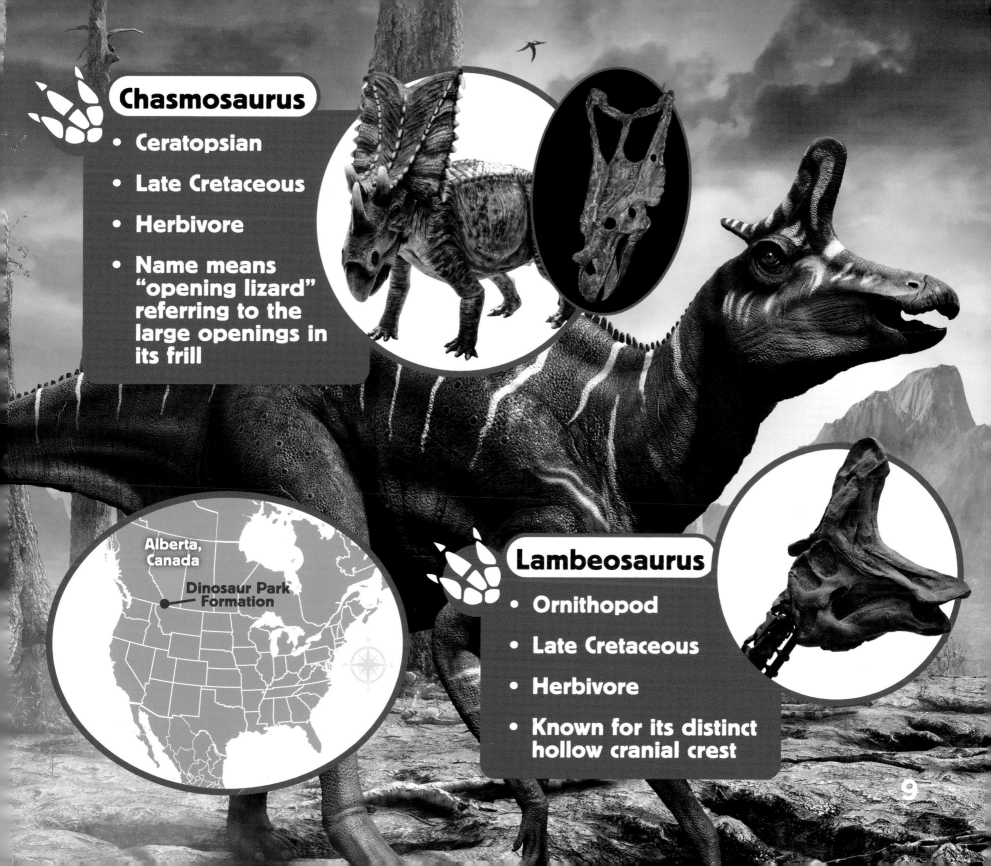

Chasmosaurus

- Ceratopsian
- Late Cretaceous
- Herbivore
- Name means "opening lizard" referring to the large openings in its frill

Alberta, Canada

Dinosaur Park Formation

Lambeosaurus

- Ornithopod
- Late Cretaceous
- Herbivore
- Known for its distinct hollow cranial crest

9

Hell Creek Formation

The Hell Creek Formation stretches across the Northwestern United States. One of the most complete Edmontosaurus fossil was found there.

Edmontosaurus

- Ornithopod
- Late Cretaceous
- Herbivore
- Could walk on 2 or 4 feet
- As long as 3 SUVs

11

Woodbury Formation

The Woodbury Formation is in New Jersey. A fossil discovered there is famous. It was the first to be mounted and shown in public.

Hadrosaurus

- Ornithopod
- Late Cretaceous
- Herbivore
- Discovered in 1858

New Jersey

13

Big Bend

Texas's Big Bend has big dinosaurs! Alamosaurus is the largest known North American dinosaur.

Big Bend

Texas

Alamosaurus

- Sauropod

- Late Cretaceous

- Herbivore

- Nearly the length of a Boeing 757-500 airplane

15

Giant **pterosaur** fossils were found there too. The remains belonged to one of the biggest flying animals to ever live.

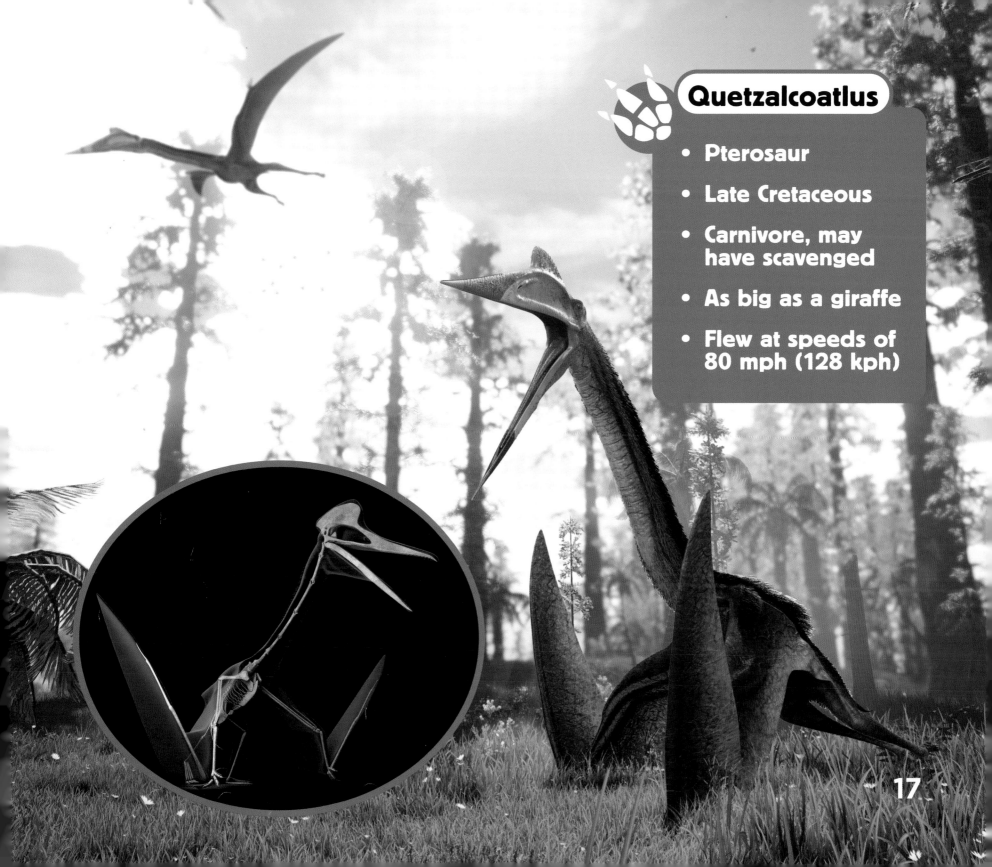

Quetzalcoatlus

- Pterosaur

- Late Cretaceous

- Carnivore, may have scavenged

- As big as a giraffe

- Flew at speeds of 80 mph (128 kph)

17

Morrison Formation

The Morrison Formation holds the most fossils in North America. Many stegosaurus remains are buried there.

MT ND
ID WY SD
UT CO NE
KS
AZ NM OK
TX

Stegosaurus

- **Stegosaurian**
- **Late Jurassic**
- **Herbivore**

19

Large sauropods are also common in the formation. Their largest **predator** is found there too.

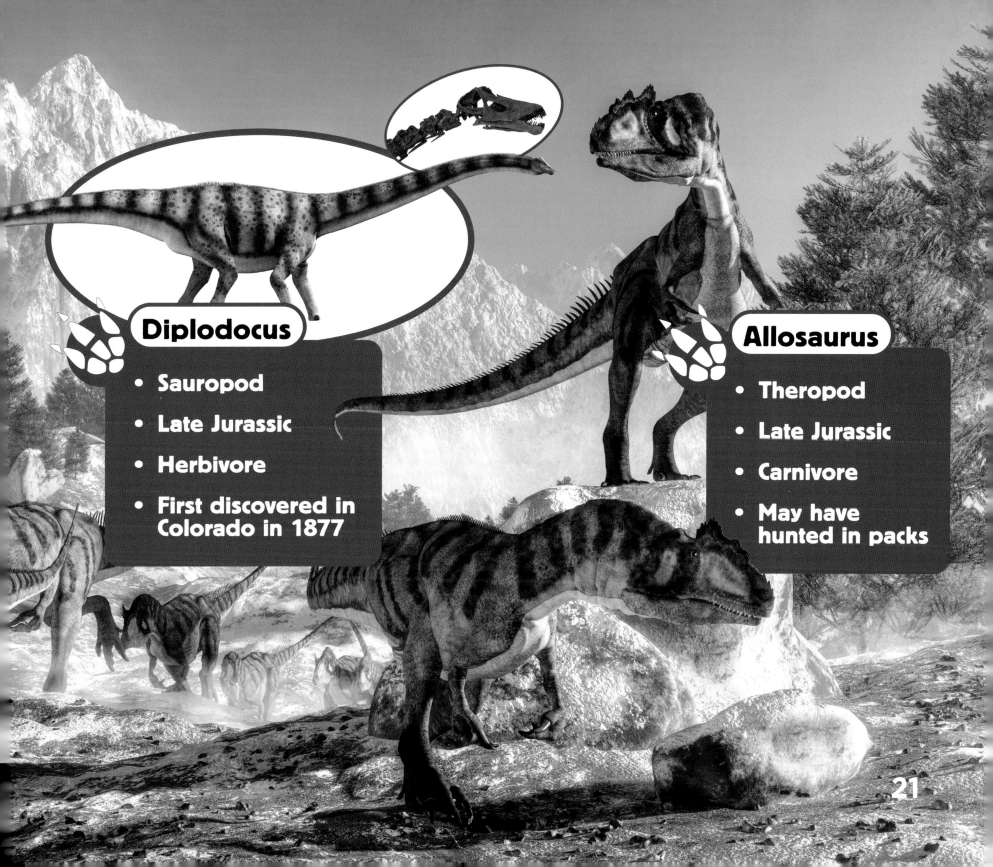

Diplodocus

- Sauropod
- Late Jurassic
- Herbivore
- First discovered in Colorado in 1877

Allosaurus

- Theropod
- Late Jurassic
- Carnivore
- May have hunted in packs

21

Some Major Dinosaur Groups

Ankylosauria
- Four-legged
- Heavily armored
- Tank-like
- Some members had clubbed tails
- Herbivores

Ceratopsia
- Four-legged
- Solidly built
- Enormous skulls
- Long horns
- Sharp beaks
- Herbivores

Ornithischia

Ornithopoda
- Two-legged
- Beaked
- Had cheek teeth
- Herbivores

Stegosauria
- Four-legged
- Small heads
- Heavy, bony plates with sharp spikes down the backbone
- Herbivores

Sauropoda
- Four-legged
- Very large
- Long necks and tails
- Small heads
- Herbivores

Saurichia

Theropoda
- Two-legged
- From small and delicate to very large in size
- Small arms
- Carnivores and omnivores

Glossary

carnivore – an animal that eats the flesh of other animals.

herbivore – an animal that feeds only on plants.

omnivore – an animal that eats both plants and other animals.

predator – an animal that hunts other animals for food.

pterosaur – a flying reptile that lived alongside dinosaurs. It had wings and a birdlike beak.

rock formation – a large body of rock that has a consistent set of physical characteristics that make it standout from other bodies of rock nearby.

23

Index

Alamosaurus 14, 15

Allosaurus 20, 21

Canada 8

Chasmosaurus 9

Diplodocus 20, 21

Edmontosaurus 10, 11

Hadrosaurus 12, 13

Lambeosaurus 9

New Jersey 12

Quetzalcoatlus 16, 17

Stegosaurus 18, 19

Texas 14, 16

United States 10, 12, 14, 16, 18, 20

Abdo Kids
ONLINE
FREE! ONLINE MULTIMEDIA RESOURCES

Visit **abdokids.com**
to access crafts, games,
videos, and more!

Use Abdo Kids code

DDK9483

or scan this QR code!